Progress-Monitoring Assessments

Grade 4

HOUGHTON MIFFLIN HARCOURT

Contents

Progress-Monitoring Assessments

The *Houghton Mifflin Harcourt Journeys* program provides intervention to support students who are having difficulty reading. The Progress-Monitoring Assessments provide biweekly checks on students' progress. The fifteen oral tests are administered individually and assess students' growth in reading skills.

Purpose of the Progress-Monitoring Assessments

- To check on a student's growth or problems in learning skills and vocabulary
- To target learning gaps by using these test results combined with test results from the core instructional program

Skills Tested in the Intervention Program

Tested skills include
- Fluency (accuracy and rate)
- Comprehension
- Target Vocabulary

Test Organization

- Fifteen biweekly assessments are provided on blackline masters.

- Each assessment includes the student's test followed by the teacher's test form with questions and scoring information.

- This booklet provides directions for administering and scoring each test. Also included are guidelines for interpreting test results and reproducible record-keeping forms.

Progress-Monitoring Assessments have two sections:

- Passages for students to read aloud, which include selected Target Vocabulary from the previous two lessons

- Oral questions that check comprehension and vocabulary

Fluency goals are based on below grade-level norms in order to measure progress with intervention instruction. Use grade-level fluency norms, along with observation and program assessment, to determine whether or not a student can transition out of intervention.

Administering the Assessments

Administer each assessment orally to individuals approximately every two weeks. The test should take three to five minutes.

Prepare one student test form and a teacher's test form for each student being tested. Use it to record the student's responses and scores.

Materials Needed

- Student's test form
- Teacher's test form (one per student being tested)
- Stopwatch, watch, or clock with a second hand
- Clipboard (optional)

Keep in Mind

- Find a quiet area to conduct the test.

- Explain the task, and let the student know that you will be taking notes as he or she reads a passage aloud.

- Tell the student to read at his or her usual pace and not rush through the reading.

- Wait until the student has left to score and analyze the results.

To administer the oral reading section:

- Have a clock or watch with a second hand or a stopwatch available to time the student's reading.

- Explain that the test has two parts. First, you'll listen to the student read a passage aloud. Then you'll ask questions about it. If a student has trouble decoding a word, remind him or her to use the Decoding Strategy.

- Time the student's reading for 30 seconds.

- Record errors by drawing a line through mispronounced or omitted words. Write in words that the student inserts. Mark self-corrections with SC above the word.

- Mark an X on the last word that the student reads at 30 seconds.

- Allow the student to finish reading the entire passage.

To administer the comprehension and vocabulary questions:

- At the end of the reading ask the questions provided, and have the student respond orally.

- Give the student a reasonable time to respond. Use the rubric on the teacher's test form to evaluate the response. Record a number.

Scoring the Assessments

1. Determine the student's fluency score; record it on the teacher's test form.

- Count mispronunciations, additions, and omissions as errors.

- Do not count repetitions or self-corrections as errors.

- Subtract errors from total number of words read to get the total number of words read correctly in 30 seconds.

- Multiply the words read correctly in 30 seconds times 2 to determine the number of words read correctly in one minute (WCPM).

2. Calculate the student's comprehension and vocabulary score. Record it on the teacher's test form.

- Evaluate the completeness of the student's answers. Give partial credit for an answer with too few details or one that required prompting. Record the number.

- Add the vocabulary and comprehension scores together and enter the total score.

How to Score Comprehension and Vocabulary Questions
2 = full credit answer
1 = partial credit answer
0 = incorrect/unanswered

3. Compare the scores and goals. Decide whether the student should move ahead or needs reteaching.

4. Record each student's scores across test periods on the Progress-Monitoring Chart. See the blackline masters on pages xi–xii.

Interpreting Test Results

Use progress-monitoring test results, observations, and grade-level assessment results to make decisions about future intervention. They will help you:

- determine if the student needs additional intervention or can be transitioned back to core instruction only

- evaluate the overall effectiveness of intervention strategies by noting sufficient progress and learning

- adjust skill instruction to address specific learning gaps

Consider how a student's scores compare to the goals. Decide if the student is benefiting from additional intervention.

☐ **Move Ahead** The student met goals for both sections.	☐ **Needs Reteaching** The student did not meet goals for one or both sections.

Adjusting Instruction

Evaluate a student's errors and responses to identify problem areas and starting points for reteaching, review, and extra practice.

- **To build accuracy** Analyze the types of errors in oral reading. Reteach target phonics/decoding skills as needed, and provide appropriate word lists for more practice. If a student is making many self-corrections, try recording the student's reading and play it back so he or she can hear his or her own reading.

- **To build fluency** Provide familiar texts at a student's independent reading level for repeated or coached readings.

- **To build comprehension** Emphasize understanding the meaning of text. Take turns with students modeling how to apply comprehension strategies to different texts.

Test Results and Regrouping

Students in Strategic Intervention take part in the core instruction, activities, and assessments from *Houghton Mifflin Harcourt Journeys*. Test results from the Progress-Monitoring Assessments and Quick Check observations from the lessons indicate whether a student is benefiting from Strategic Intervention. Test results from other *Journeys* assessments provide data to help determine how to regroup students periodically.

Using *Houghton Mifflin Harcourt Journeys* Assessments	
Core Instructional Program Weekly and Unit Tests Benchmark and Fluency Tests	• Measure grade-level skill mastery and growth. • Use cut-off scores and professional judgment to regroup students who need intervention support.
Strategic Intervention Biweekly Progress-Monitoring Assessments	• Measures a student's gains as a result of Strategic Intervention instruction. • Use progress-monitoring results, observations, and program assessments to determine if a student needs additional Strategic Intervention or should transition out of intervention or to more intensive intervention. • If a student has not performed adequately (met goals) for two or three consecutive assessments, consult with colleagues to decide whether to increase the intensity of intervention.

Progress-Monitoring Chart

Name _____

Teacher _____

School year _____

Enter scores from test forms.

For Lessons	Date Given	FLUENCY — Enter Words Correct per Minute (WCPM)	COMPREHENSION and VOCABULARY — Enter Score Goal: 4/6	ACTIONS (Check One)		COMMENTS
				Move Ahead	Needs Reteaching	
1–2						
3–4						
5–6						
7–8						
9–10						
11–12						
13–14						

Progress Monitoring
© Houghton Mifflin Harcourt Publishing Company

Grade 4

Progress-Monitoring Chart

Name _____ Teacher _____ School year _____

Enter scores from test forms.

For Lessons	Date Given	FLUENCY Enter Words Correct per Minute (WCPM)	COMPREHENSION and VOCABULARY Enter Score Goal: 4/6	ACTIONS (Check One) Move Ahead	Needs Reteaching	COMMENTS
15–16						
17–18						
19–20						
21–22						
23–24						
25–26						
27–28						
29–30						

Amy and Tom

Amy and Tom are sister and brother. They take turns when they play games. Sometimes it is easy to take turns and sometimes it is not.

Dad asks the children if they want to go to the store. Amy and Tom race to the car. They each try to be first to get in the front seat. Dad asks whose turn it is to ride up front. Amy and Tom both say, "Mine!" But Dad says it is Amy's turn. This puts Tom in a bad mood.

When Tom and Amy get home from the store, they want to watch a TV show. They both want to pick the show. Dad asks whose turn it is. Tom and Amy both say, "Mine!" Dad tells Tom to pick the show. Amy thinks this is an injustice!

After the show, Mom asks whose turn it is to wash the numerous dishes in the sink. Amy says, "His!" Tom says, "Hers!" Mom and Dad laugh.

Amy and Tom

Amy and Tom are sister and brother. They take turns when they play games. Sometimes it is easy to take turns and sometimes it is not. 3 12 22 29

Dad asks the children if they want to go to the store. Amy and Tom race to the car. They each try to be first to get in the front seat. Dad asks whose turn it is to ride up front. Amy and Tom both say, "Mine!" But Dad says it is Amy's turn. This puts Tom in a bad mood. 40 51 63 75 85 90

When Tom and Amy get home from the store, they want to watch a TV show. They both want to pick the show. Dad asks whose turn it is. Tom and Amy both say, "Mine!" Dad tells Tom to pick the show. Amy thinks this is an injustice! 99 110 121 131 138

After the show, Mom asks whose turn it is to wash the numerous dishes in the sink. Amy says, "His!" Tom says, "Hers!" Mom and Dad laugh. 148 157 165

Comprehension and Vocabulary Questions

1. *Why does Dad have to decide whose turn it is to sit in the front seat or pick a TV show?* (Amy and Tom have trouble taking turns and they argue about it.)

2. *Why does Amy think that her father's decision was an <u>injustice</u>?* (She thought it was unfair that Dad said it was Tom's turn to pick the TV show.)

3. *Why do Mom and Dad laugh at the end of the story?* (Amy and Tom always want to be picked except when it is time to wash the dishes.)

Fluency Score	Comprehension/Vocabulary Score	How to Score Questions

Total words correctly read in 30 seconds _____
 	
        X 2
 	
 Score _____
 Goal 41–61 WCPM
	1. _____
	
	 2. _____
	
	 3. _____ Score _____ /6
	          Goal = 4/6
		2 = full credit answer
		 1 = partial credit answer
		 0 = incorrect/unanswered

☐ **Move Ahead** The student met goals for both sections. | ☐ **Needs Reteaching** The student did not meet goals for one or both sections.

The King of Insects

Beetles may be the kings of insects. There are more beetles than any other kind of insect.

Almost 400,000 kinds of beetles live on Earth. The biggest beetles are six inches long! That is very long. Some beetles are brown. Some are black. Some are green. Green beetles are very pretty. A ladybug is a beetle. You may have held one in your hand.

People do many things with beetles. Ladybugs are one kind of beetle. People with gardens buy boxes of ladybugs. Ladybugs are welcome in gardens. They assist in eating insects that hurt plants. This is good for the garden. It helps the plants grow. Other people keep beetles as pets. In some places, people eat beetles.

If we included all of the animals in the world in a line, every fourth one would be a beetle. That is a lot of beetles! This is why the beetle is called the king of insects.

The King of Insects

Beetles may be the kings of insects. There are   13
more beetles than any other kind of insect.   21

Almost 400,000 kinds of beetles live on Earth.   29
The biggest beetles are six inches long! That is very   39
long. Some beetles are brown. Some are black. Some   48
are green. Green beetles are very pretty. A ladybug   57
is a beetle. You may have held one in your hand.   68

People do many things with beetles. Ladybugs   75
are one kind of beetle. People with gardens buy   84
boxes of ladybugs. Ladybugs are welcome in   91
gardens. They assist in eating insects that hurt plants.   100
This is good for the garden. It helps the plants grow.   111
Other people keep beetles as pets. In some places,   120
people eat beetles.   123

If we included all of the animals in the world in a   135
line, every fourth one would be a beetle. That is a lot   147
of beetles! This is why the beetle is called the king   158
of insects.   160

4

GO ON

Comprehension and Vocabulary Questions

1. *What would be another title for this passage?* (An Unusual Insect; Beetles Are Important Bugs; All About Beetles)

2. *How do beetles <u>assist</u> people?* (They eat insects that hurt garden plants. This helps plants grow.)

3. *Why is the beetle called the king of insects?* (There are more beetles in the world than any other kind of insect.)

Fluency Score	Comprehension / Vocabulary Score	How to Score Questions
Total words correctly read in 30 seconds _____ X 2 Score _____ Goal 41–61 WCPM	1. _____ 2. _____ 3. _____ Score ____ /6 Goal = 4/6	2 = full credit answer 1 = partial credit answer 0 = incorrect/unanswered

☐ **Move Ahead** The student met goals for both sections.

☐ **Needs Reteaching** The student did not meet goals for one or both sections.

Jean and Ben

It was such a nice day that Jean had a yearning to go to the park. She packed a picnic. Then she called her dog, Ben.

"Let's go to the park, Ben. I packed a picnic for us." Ben came running.

"I love the park," Ben said. "What did you pack for me to eat?"

"I packed your favorite dog food," answered Jean.

"This is going to be a great day!" said Ben. He put on his sunglasses. "I can hardly wait to go down the slide. And I'll push you on the swing."

Ben ran to get some things to take to the park. He got his best ball and a good book to read.

"Ben, you don't need all that!" Jean said.

"Yes, I do!" Ben answered. He refused to put them back.

"Okay, but you forgot the most important thing," Jean said.

"My leash! I'll get it!" cried Ben. He knew it would be a memorable day.

Jean and Ben

	3
It was such a nice day that Jean had a yearning	14
to go to the park. She packed a picnic. Then she	25
called her dog, Ben.	29
"Let's go to the park, Ben. I packed a picnic for	40
us." Ben came running.	44
"I love the park," Ben said. "What did you pack	54
for me to eat?"	58
"I packed your favorite dog food," answered	65
Jean.	66
"This is going to be a great day!" said Ben. He	77
put on his sunglasses. "I can hardly wait to go down	88
the slide. And I'll push you on the swing."	97
Ben ran to get some things to take to the park.	108
He got his best ball and a good book to read.	119
"Ben, you don't need all that!" Jean said.	127
"Yes, I do!" Ben answered. He refused to put	136
them back.	138
"Okay, but you forgot the most important thing,"	146
Jean said.	148
"My leash! I'll get it!" cried Ben. He knew it	158
would be a memorable day.	163

GO ON

Name _____ Date _____

Comprehension and Vocabulary Questions

1. *Why does Jean have a <u>yearning</u> to go to the park?* (It is a nice day and she wants to spend it outside at the park.)

2. *How is Ben different from other dogs?* (He is able to talk, he can read a book, and he plays in the park.)

3. *What would be a better title for this story?* (Ben the Amazing Dog; Ben the Talking Dog)

Fluency Score	Comprehension / Vocabulary Score	How to Score Questions
Total words correctly read in 30 seconds _____ X 2 Score _____ Goal 41–61 WCPM	1. _____ 2. _____ 3. _____ Score ___ /6 Goal = 4/6	2 = full credit answer 1 = partial credit answer 0 = incorrect/unanswered
☐ **Move Ahead** The student met goals for both sections.	☐ **Needs Reteaching** The student did not meet goals for one or both sections.	

The Park

The park is a glorious place to go in the winter. When the pond freezes, it is a good place to ice skate. There is a schedule for skating times.

When it snows, bring your sled. The hill is a good place for sledding. The snow on the hill is soft and deep. Be careful around the trees. You do not want to hit one!

Sometimes there are children sledding on the hill. They wear hats and boots to stay warm. Their sleds are red, green, blue, and yellow. There are so many colors! Sledding is fun for children. It is a thrilling ride to go down the hill!

Right after the snow falls, the park is very quiet. You could hear a pin drop. The snow helps to make it quiet. But if you listen, you might hear a woodpecker pecking an old tree. It is looking for bugs to eat. A busy woodpecker is very noisy!

The Park

The park is a glorious place to go in the winter.   13

When the pond freezes, it is a good place to ice   24

skate. There is a schedule for skating times.   32

When it snows, bring your sled. The hill is a good   43

place for sledding. The snow on the hill is soft and   54

deep. Be careful around the trees. You do not want   64

to hit one!   67

Sometimes there are children sledding on the   74

hill. They wear hats and boots to stay warm. Their   84

sleds are red, green, blue, and yellow. There are   93

so many colors! Sledding is fun for children. It is a   104

thrilling ride to go down the hill!   111

Right after the snow falls, the park is very   120

quiet. You could hear a pin drop. The snow helps   130

to make it quiet. But if you listen, you might hear   141

a woodpecker pecking an old tree. It is looking for   151

bugs to eat. A busy woodpecker is very noisy!   160

GO ON

Comprehension and Vocabulary Questions

1. *Where does this passage take place?* (It takes place in the park in the winter.)

2. *How is the park a* <u>glorious</u> *place in the winter?* (There are many ways to have fun in the park in the winter.)

3. *What can you do in the park in the winter?* (You can ice skate and go sledding.)

Fluency Score	Comprehension/Vocabulary Score	How to Score Questions
Total words correctly read in 30 seconds _____ X 2	1. _____	2 = full credit answer
	2. _____	1 = partial credit answer
Score _____ Goal 41–61 WCPM	3. _____ Score ____/6 Goal = 4/6	0 = incorrect/unanswered

☐ **Move Ahead** The student met goals for both sections. ☐ **Needs Reteaching** The student did not meet goals for one or both sections.

The Mouse House

In class, Mrs. Hill told us we had to "build a better mouse house." We had one week to do it. I used a big box. I put air holes in the top for my mouse, Jim. Then I made a small door for the house that moved up and down.

I put my pet mouse into his new house and took him to school. I did not ask Mrs. Hill for permission to bring Jim. The class was quiet as Mrs. Hill walked around the room. She looked at all of the houses. When she came to mine, she opened the door. Out came Jim! He landed on the floor and ran under her desk. That is when I found out I was the only one who brought a real mouse!

It took the class twenty minutes to catch Jim. I knew I had to apologize, but it was fun catching Jim. Mrs. Hill gave me a good grade. She said she liked Jim and insisted that I bring him back.

The Mouse House

	3

In class, Mrs. Hill told us we had to "build a | 14

better mouse house." We had one week to do it. | 24

I used a big box. I put air holes in the top for my | 38

mouse, Jim. Then I made a small door for the house | 49

that moved up and down. | 54

I put my pet mouse into his new house and took | 65

him to school. I did not ask Mrs. Hill for permission | 76

to bring Jim. The class was quiet as Mrs. Hill walked | 87

around the room. She looked at all of the houses. | 97

When she came to mine, she opened the door. Out | 107

came Jim! He landed on the floor and ran under her | 118

desk. That is when I found out I was the only one | 130

who brought a real mouse! | 135

It took the class twenty minutes to catch Jim. | 144

I knew I had to apologize, but it was fun catching | 155

Jim. Mrs. Hill gave me a good grade. She said she | 166

liked Jim and insisted that I bring him back. | 175

GO ON

Comprehension and Vocabulary Questions

1. *What does Mrs. Hill ask her students to do?* (She asks the class to build a house small enough for a mouse.)

2. *Who is Jim in this story?* (Jim is a mouse.)

3. *Why would the student need the teacher's <u>permission</u> to bring Jim to school?* (He was not supposed to bring a real mouse to school and he should have asked the teacher first.)

Fluency Score	Comprehension / Vocabulary Score	How to Score Questions
Total words correctly read in 30 seconds _____ X 2 Score _____ Goal 41–61 WCPM	1. _____ 2. _____ 3. _____ Score _____ /6 Goal = 4/6	2 = full credit answer 1 = partial credit answer 0 = incorrect/unanswered

☐ **Move Ahead** The student met goals for both sections.

☐ **Needs Reteaching** The student did not meet goals for one or both sections.

Pigeons

Another name for a pigeon is a rock dove. Pigeons belong to the same bird family as doves. Doves are clean and very pretty. But pigeons are not.

If you live in a city, you have probably seen pigeons in parks and other places where people eat lunch. These pigeons are looking for food. The presence of so many pigeons in one place is not a good thing. In some cities, the return of hawks has cut down the number of pigeons.

Some people teach pigeons to fly home from many miles away. These pigeons are called homing pigeons. They can carry messages or other possessions. People think that the sun helps the pigeons know which way to fly.

Passenger pigeons once lived in North America. As people moved west, they hunted these birds. By 1880, most passenger pigeons were gone. The last one died in a zoo in 1914. If people could have predicted that there would be no more passenger pigeons, then maybe they would not have hunted them.

Name _____ Date _____

Pigeons

Another name for a pigeon is a rock dove.	10
Pigeons belong to the same bird family as doves.	19
Doves are clean and very pretty. But pigeons are	28
not.	29
If you live in a city, you have probably seen	39
pigeons in parks and other places where people	47
eat lunch. These pigeons are looking for food. The	56
presence of so many pigeons in one place is not a	67
good thing. In some cities, the return of hawks has	77
cut down the number of pigeons.	83
Some people teach pigeons to fly home	90
from many miles away. These pigeons are called	98
homing pigeons. They can carry messages or other	106
possessions. People think that the sun helps the	114
pigeons know which way to fly.	120
Passenger pigeons once lived in North America.	127
As people moved west, they hunted these birds.	135
By 1880, most passenger pigeons were gone. The	143
last one died in a zoo in 1914. If people could	154
have predicted that there would be no more	162
passenger pigeons, then maybe they would not	169
have hunted them.	172

The number 1 appears at the top right of the passage.

GO ON

Comprehension and Vocabulary Questions

1. *Where would be a good place to see pigeons?* (You can find pigeons in a park or anywhere people are eating because pigeons are always looking for food.)

2. *What makes homing pigeons so special?* (They can fly home from many miles away, carry messages, and use the sun to help them fly.)

3. *What might have happened if people could have <u>predicted</u> that there would be no more passenger pigeons?* (People wouldn't have hunted them and made them go away.)

Fluency Score	**Comprehension/Vocabulary Score**	**How to Score Questions**
Total words correctly read in 30 seconds _____ X 2 Score _____ Goal 62–82 WCPM	1. _____ 2. _____ 3. _____ Score _____ /6 Goal = 4/6	2 = full credit answer 1 = partial credit answer 0 = incorrect/unanswered

☐ **Move Ahead** The student met goals for both sections.

☐ **Needs Reteaching** The student did not meet goals for one or both sections.

Wanda's Swamp

Wanda likes to visit the swamp. A swamp is a place that is very wet. Wanda's dad takes her around the swamp in his boat. They float under the big willow trees and gum trees.

Many animals live in the swamp. Wanda stays alert in the boat. She looks out for cottonmouth snakes. She knows they are very dangerous. Wanda's dad likes to watch for birds. He points out the different birds in the sky. Many are social birds and stay together in groups. There are many animals in the swamp that they never see. The fox only comes out at night, and the bobcat stays away from people. There are fish in the water, but the water is too dark to see them.

From the boat, Wanda can see turtles. The turtles lie in the sun and do not move. They look like they are stranded on the rocks. But Wanda knows they can swim to land. Once, Wanda saw a raccoon catching a fish. But the most exciting day at the swamp was when she saw two bear cubs running between the trees!

Wanda's Swamp

 Wanda likes to visit the swamp. A swamp is a 2
place that is very wet. Wanda's dad takes her around 12
the swamp in his boat. They float under the big 22
willow trees and gum trees. 32

 Many animals live in the swamp. Wanda stays 37
alert in the boat. She looks out for cottonmouth 45
snakes. She knows they are very dangerous. 54
Wanda's dad likes to watch for birds. He points out 61
the different birds in the sky. Many are social birds 71
and stay together in groups. There are many animals 81
in the swamp that they never see. The fox only 90
comes out at night, and the bobcat stays away from 100
people. There are fish in the water, but the water is 110
too dark to see them. 121

 From the boat, Wanda can see turtles. The 125
turtles lie in the sun and do not move. They look 134
like they are stranded on the rocks. But Wanda 145
knows they can swim to land. Once, Wanda saw a 154
raccoon catching a fish. But the most exciting day at 164
the swamp was when she saw two bear cubs running 174
between the trees! 184
  187

GO ON

Comprehension and Vocabulary Questions

1. *Why does Wanda like to visit the swamp?* (She likes to look at all of the animals in the swamp.)

2. *Why does Wanda stay <u>alert</u> in the boat?* (She is watching for different types of animals, especially dangerous ones.)

3. *What kinds of animals has Wanda seen at the swamp?* (She has seen birds, turtles, a raccoon, and two bear cubs.)

Fluency Score	Comprehension / Vocabulary Score		How to Score Questions
Total words correctly read in 30 seconds _____ X 2 Score _____ Goal 62–82 WCPM	1. _____ 2. _____ 3. _____	Score _____ /6 Goal = 4/6	2 = full credit answer 1 = partial credit answer 0 = incorrect/unanswered
☐ **Move Ahead** The student met goals for both sections.		☐ **Needs Reteaching** The student did not meet goals for one or both sections.	

The Land of the Midnight Sun

Iceland is a country that is also a large island. It is a great place to see. It is very far north in the North Atlantic Ocean. For two months in the winter, it is dark all the time. There is daylight for only four to six hours a day. But for a month in the summer, it is light all the time and there is no night at all. That is why some people call Iceland "The Land of the Midnight Sun."

Even though Iceland is very far north, it is not as cold as you might think. Most people in Iceland live near the sea. Warm winds from the sea affect the land and keep it from getting very cold. The winds keep the island from being hit directly with the cold air. The summers in Iceland are cool, too. It feels more like spring than the hot summers we are used to.

Iceland is a wonderful place to visit. It is very pretty, and there are many species of animals that live there. You should think about going to see this island soon!

The Land of the Midnight Sun

Iceland is a country that is also a large island.
It is a great place to see. It is very far north in the
North Atlantic Ocean. For two months in the winter,
it is dark all the time. There is daylight for only four
to six hours a day. But for a month in the summer, it
is light all the time and there is no night at all. That
is why some people call Iceland "The Land of the
Midnight Sun."

Even though Iceland is very far north, it is not as
cold as you might think. Most people in Iceland live
near the sea. Warm winds from the sea affect the
land and keep it from getting very cold. The winds
keep the island from being hit directly with the cold
air. The summers in Iceland are cool, too. It feels
more like spring than the hot summers we are used to.

Iceland is a wonderful place to visit. It is very
pretty, and there are many species of animals that
live there. You should think about going to see this
island soon!

6
16
30
39
51
64
77
87
89
100
110
120
130
140
150
161
171
180
190
192

GO ON

Name _____ Date _____

Comprehension and Vocabulary Questions

1. *What details from the passage support the idea that Iceland is a wonderful place?* (It does not get very cold or very hot. It is very pretty. There are many types of animals.)

2. *How is winter different from summer in Iceland?* (It stays dark most of the time in winter and light most of the time in summer.)

3. *How do the winds from the sea* <u>affect</u> *Iceland?* (The warm winds keep the land from getting hit with cold air; they cause the land to stay warmer than you would think it would be so far north.)

Fluency Score	Comprehension / Vocabulary Score	How to Score Questions

Total words correctly read in 30 seconds _____
X 2
 	
Score _____
Goal 62–82 WCPM
	1. _____
	
	2. _____
	
	3. _____
	       Score _____ /6
	       Goal = 4/6
		2 = full credit answer
		1 = partial credit answer
		0 = incorrect/unanswered

☐ **Move Ahead** The student met goals for both sections.	☐ **Needs Reteaching** The student did not meet goals for one or both sections.	

Mike's Idea

Mike's class wanted to do something special for the children at the hospital. They decided to raise money to buy books. They would have a cookie sale at school. Everyone would bring cookies to sell.

When he got home, Mike asked his mother for help making cookies. She patiently reminded him that she had to go to work soon.

Mike asked his father for help. His father wanted to help, but he had promised to help Mike's sister build her science project.

Finally, Mike decided to count his money. He had been saving to buy a new model to build. He could buy cookies, but then he would have to wait even longer to get the model.

Then Mike devised an idea. He called his pal Tran. They could make cookies together! Tran's grandfather would help them. Mike took sugar and flour to Tran's house. Mike and Tran and Tran's grandfather made cookies. The next day, the class sold cookies. To reward themselves, they used the money to buy ten books for the children at the hospital. Next time they hope to buy even more.

Name ______________________________ Date ____________

Mike's Idea 2

Mike's class wanted to do something special for 10
the children at the hospital. They decided to raise 19
money to buy books. They would have a cookie sale 29
at school. Everyone would bring cookies to sell. 37

When he got home, Mike asked his mother for 46
help making cookies. She patiently reminded him 53
that she had to go to work soon. 61

Mike asked his father for help. His father wanted 70
to help, but he had promised to help Mike's sister 80
build her science project. 84

Finally, Mike decided to count his money. He 92
had been saving to buy a new model to build. He 103
could buy cookies, but then he would have to wait 113
even longer to get the model. 119

Then Mike devised an idea. He called his pal 128
Tran. They could make cookies together! Tran's 135
grandfather would help them. Mike took sugar 142
and flour to Tran's house. Mike and Tran and Tran's 152
grandfather made cookies. The next day, the class 160
sold cookies. To reward themselves, they used the 168
money to buy ten books for the children at the 178
hospital. Next time they hope to buy even more. 187

GO ON

Comprehension and Vocabulary Questions

1. *What is Mike's idea?* (Mike wants to raise money by having a cookie sale, so he asks everyone in the school to bring in cookies.)

2. *What happens when Mike <u>devises</u> an idea?* (He comes up with a plan to make cookies with Tran.)

3. *What happens when Mike's class sells the cookies?* (They use the money they have raised to buy books for the hospital.)

Fluency Score	Comprehension/Vocabulary Score	How to Score Questions

Total words correctly read in 30 seconds _____
 	
          X 2
 	
Score _____
Goal 62–82 WCPM
	1. _____
	
	2. _____
	
	3. _____ Score ____ /6
	              Goal = 4/6
		2 = full credit answer
		1 = partial credit answer
		0 = incorrect/unanswered

☐ **Move Ahead** The student met goals for both sections.	☐ **Needs Reteaching** The student did not meet goals for one or both sections.	

Symbols of Freedom

How many different kinds of eagles do you think live in the world? If you guessed about sixty, you would be right. Some kinds of eagles are large and some are small. Some have had to overcome many problems to still be here. Most are strong for their size. Some are even strong enough to lift food that is almost as heavy as they are!

Eagles have been used as symbols of freedom. Some people call them the "king of birds" because of their brave, proud looks. These birds seem to know what their duty is. In 1782, this country chose the bald eagle as its national bird. The bald eagle has had a lot of publicity since then.

Bald eagles are large birds. They can weigh from eight to thirteen pounds. These great birds can have wings that spread as much as seven feet across! Their heads are covered with white feathers, making them look "bald" from a distance. So now you know how they got their name! The bald eagle is a very good choice for a national bird.

Symbols of Freedom

How many different kinds of eagles do you think	12
live in the world? If you guessed about sixty, you	22
would be right. Some kinds of eagles are large and	32
some are small. Some have had to overcome many	41
problems to still be here. Most are strong for their	51
size. Some are even strong enough to lift food that is	62
almost as heavy as they are!	68
Eagles have been used as symbols of freedom.	76
Some people call them the "king of birds" because of	86
their brave, proud looks. These birds seem to know	95
what their duty is. In 1782, this country chose the	105
bald eagle as its national bird. The bald eagle has had	116
a lot of publicity since then.	122
Bald eagles are large birds. They can weigh from	131
eight to thirteen pounds. These great birds can have	140
wings that spread as much as seven feet across! Their	150
heads are covered with white feathers, making them	158
look "bald" from a distance. So now you know how	168
they got their name! The bald eagle is a very good	179
choice for a national bird.	184

The title "Symbols of Freedom" appears above with a **3** to its right.

GO ON

Comprehension and Vocabulary Questions

1. *What is the main idea of the passage?* (Eagles are interesting birds that are symbols of freedom.)

2. *In what way have eagles overcome their problems?* (They are strong birds that have found a way to stay alive. They are able to lift food that weighs as much as they do.)

3. *Why are eagles a good choice for our national bird?* (They are large, strong, and proud.)

Fluency Score	Comprehension / Vocabulary Score	How to Score Questions
Total words correctly read in 30 seconds _____ X 2	1. _____	2 = full credit answer
	2. _____	1 = partial credit answer
Score _____ Goal 62–82 WCPM	3. _____ Score _____ /6 Goal = 4/6	0 = incorrect/unanswered
☐ **Move Ahead** The student met goals for both sections.	☐ **Needs Reteaching** The student did not meet goals for one or both sections.	

Going Fishing

One sunny afternoon, Sam and his grandfather went fishing. They walked through the woods to the edge of the lake. Sam found a log for them to sit on. His grandfather set up their poles and put worms on the hooks. While they sat on the log fishing, Sam's grandfather told interesting stories.

Soon, Sam had a bite on his line. He reeled the line in and caught his first fish. Sam was so excited that he almost fell into the water. His grandfather helped him get the fish off the hook and put it in the bucket promptly. Together they sat talking and fishing until huge black clouds blocked the sun.

"Uh-oh, looks like a storm is coming," said Sam's grandfather. He was about to suggest they leave when thunder rumbled in the distance. Rain was falling across the lake.

They packed their things. As they walked back through the woods, the rain began to pour down.

"This looks serious!" said Sam's grandfather.

When they got to the car, they were soaking wet. Sam was cold, but he was happy. He could appreciate the time he spent fishing, even though it was short.

Going Fishing 2

One sunny afternoon, Sam and his grandfather 9
went fishing. They walked through the woods to the 18
edge of the lake. Sam found a log for them to sit on. 31
His grandfather set up their poles and put worms on 41
the hooks. While they sat on the log fishing, Sam's 51
grandfather told interesting stories. 55

Soon, Sam had a bite on his line. He reeled the 66
line in and caught his first fish. Sam was so excited 77
that he almost fell into the water. His grandfather 86
helped him get the fish off the hook and put it in 98
the bucket promptly. Together they sat talking and 106
fishing until huge black clouds blocked the sun. 114

"Uh-oh, looks like a storm is coming," said Sam's 123
grandfather. He was about to suggest they leave 131
when thunder rumbled in the distance. Rain was 139
falling across the lake. 143

They packed their things. As they walked back 151
through the woods, the rain began to pour down. 160

"This looks serious!" said Sam's grandfather. 166

When they got to the car, they were soaking 175
wet. Sam was cold, but he was happy. He could 185
appreciate the time he spent fishing, even though it 194
was short. 196

GO ON

Comprehension and Vocabulary Questions

1. *What do Sam and his grandfather do at the lake?* (They fish, talk, and the grandfather tells stories.)

2. *Why does Sam get so excited that he almost falls into the water?* (He catches his first fish.)

3. *Why does Sam* <u>appreciate</u> *his day even though it rains?* (He is happy that he was able to spend time with his grandfather.)

Fluency Score	Comprehension / Vocabulary Score	How to Score Questions
Total words correctly read in 30 seconds _____ X 2	1. _____	2 = full credit answer
	2. _____	1 = partial credit answer
Score _____ Goal 79–99 WCPM	3. _____ Score ____ /6 Goal = 4/6	0 = incorrect/unanswered

☐ **Move Ahead** The student met goals for both sections.

☐ **Needs Reteaching** The student did not meet goals for one or both sections.

Crayons

Crayons are fun to use, but do you know how they are made? The first step in making crayons is to make the color. A lot of water is mixed with other materials to make each color. Then most of the water is squeezed out. What is left is a dense cake of color. There is only a little water left in it.

Next, people break up these cakes of color and put them into ovens so that the colored cakes will dry. After the cakes have suffered hours of high heat, hard lumps of color come out of the ovens. The cakes are dry and there is no moisture in them. These lumps are put in a machine that breaks them into a powder. People pour the powder into bags and send the bags to where the crayons are made.

There are big tanks of hot wax where crayons are made. This wax is added to the colored powder and then poured into crayon molds. Cold water cools the hot wax and makes it hard.

Once the wax is hard, it comes out of the molds. Paper is put around each piece and the crayons are put into boxes.

Crayons

| | 1 |

Crayons are fun to use, but do you know how | 11
they are made? The first step in making crayons is | 21
to make the color. A lot of water is mixed with other | 33
materials to make each color. Then most of the | 42
water is squeezed out. What is left is a dense cake of | 54
color. There is only a little water left in it. | 64

Next, people break up these cakes of color and | 73
put them into ovens so that the colored cakes will | 83
dry. After the cakes have suffered hours of high | 92
heat, hard lumps of color come out of the ovens. | 102
The cakes are dry and there is no moisture in them. | 113
These lumps are put in a machine that breaks them | 123
into a powder. People pour the powder into bags | 132
and send the bags to where the crayons are made. | 142

There are big tanks of hot wax where crayons are | 152
made. This wax is added to the colored powder and | 162
then poured into crayon molds. Cold water cools the | 171
hot wax and makes it hard. | 177

Once the wax is hard, it comes out of the molds. | 188
Paper is put around each piece and the crayons are | 198
put into boxes. | 201

GO ON

Comprehension and Vocabulary Questions

1. *How do crayons change from the beginning of the process to the end?* (Crayons start out as dry cakes of color that are made into powder. Then wax is added to the powder, and the mixture is poured into molds. The molds shape the colored wax into crayons.)

2. *How are crayons and cakes alike and different?* (Both are mixed with other things and baked in ovens. Cakes are put in pans and crayons are put into molds.)

3. *Why must the cakes of color have no <u>moisture</u> in them?* (They must be dry enough to break into powder.)

Fluency Score	**Comprehension / Vocabulary Score**	**How to Score Questions**
Total words correctly read in 30 seconds _____ X 2 Score _____ Goal 79–99 WCPM	1. _____ 2. _____ 3. _____ Score _____ /6 Goal = 4/6	2 = full credit answer 1 = partial credit answer 0 = incorrect/unanswered
☐ **Move Ahead** The student met goals for both sections.	☐ **Needs Reteaching** The student did not meet goals for one or both sections.	

Katie's Dog

One cold morning as Katie walked her dog, Vista, she noticed fresh tracks in the snow. A minute later, a small, peculiar dog appeared by the river. With no tag or collar, it clearly was lost. It stared hopefully at Katie and shivered in the cold. Then Vista barked, and the dog ran off. "It's much too cold for a dog to stay outside for long," Katie thought. "I've got to do something, but Vista will keep scaring it away."

So Katie headed for home. She told her mother about the lost dog, and together they returned to the river to find it. Her mother wanted to assist Katie with catching the dog because she knew how important it was to her.

Katie was almost ready to give up, but at last she spotted the dog. She called to it, but it jumped onto a rock. Katie felt like she was making progress and knelt down. The little dog leaped into her arms and began licking her face.

Katie and her mother took the dog home. Weeks later, the little dog's owner still could not be found. So that is how Dolly, the little dog, came to be part of Katie's family.

Katie's Dog

One cold morning as Katie walked her dog,   **10**
Vista, she noticed fresh tracks in the snow. A   **19**
minute later, a small, peculiar dog appeared by the   **28**
river. With no tag or collar, it clearly was lost. It   **39**
stared hopefully at Katie and shivered in the cold.   **48**
Then Vista barked, and the dog ran off. "It's much   **58**
too cold for a dog to stay outside for long," Katie   **69**
thought. "I've got to do something, but Vista will   **78**
keep scaring it away."   **82**

So Katie headed for home. She told her mother   **91**
about the lost dog, and together they returned to   **100**
the river to find it. Her mother wanted to assist   **110**
Katie with catching the dog because she knew how   **119**
important it was to her.   **124**

Katie was almost ready to give up, but at last she   **135**
spotted the dog. She called to it, but it jumped onto   **146**
a rock. Katie felt like she was making progress and   **156**
knelt down. The little dog leaped into her arms and   **166**
began licking her face.   **170**

Katie and her mother took the dog home. Weeks   **179**
later, the little dog's owner still could not be found.   **189**
So that is how Dolly, the little dog, came to be part   **201**
of Katie's family.   **204**

Comprehension and Vocabulary Questions

1. *What happens to Katie at the beginning of the story?* (She finds a lost dog and wants to take it home.)

2. *Why does Katie feel like she is making* <u>progress</u> *with catching the dog?* (The dog comes closer to her instead of running away.)

3. *What would be a better title for this story?* (Katie Finds a New Dog; How Dolly Joined the Family)

Fluency Score	Comprehension / Vocabulary Score	How to Score Questions
Total words correctly read in 30 seconds _____ X 2 Score _____ Goal 79–99 WCPM	1. _____ 2. _____ 3. _____ Score _____ /6 Goal = 4/6	2 = full credit answer 1 = partial credit answer 0 = incorrect/unanswered
☐ **Move Ahead** The student met goals for both sections.	☐ **Needs Reteaching** The student did not meet goals for one or both sections.	

Yard Sales

You have probably seen people having yard sales. They put tables in their yard. Then they put prices on things that they want to sell. They place these things on the tables for people to look at. Yard sales are a great way to clean clutter out of your house.

To have a yard sale, all you need are things that are still in good condition, but that you do not want. Do not sell things that are rare before you find out how much they are worth! Price each thing for a lot less than it would be if it were new. If you do not have enough things to sell, have a friend or neighbor join you and include their things in the sale.

You can make it easy for people to find something to buy by putting your things for sale on display in groups. Put all books in one spot and toys in another spot. You can make some signs to let people in the neighborhood know about the sale. As the sale goes on, you can lower the prices on things that are not selling. If your sale goes well, you will make some money by the end of the day!

Yard Sales

You have probably seen people having yard   2
sales. They put tables in their yard. Then they put   9
prices on things that they want to sell. They place   19
these things on the tables for people to look at.   29
Yard sales are a great way to clean clutter out of   39
your house.   50
                                                             52

To have a yard sale, all you need are things that   63
are still in good condition, but that you do not want.   74
Do not sell things that are rare before you find out   85
how much they are worth! Price each thing for a lot   96
less than it would be if it were new. If you do not   109
have enough things to sell, have a friend or neighbor   119
join you and include their things in the sale.   128

You can make it easy for people to find   137
something to buy by putting your things for sale on   147
display in groups. Put all books in one spot and toys   158
in another spot. You can make some signs to let   168
people in the neighborhood know about the sale. As   177
the sale goes on, you can lower the prices on things   188
that are not selling. If your sale goes well, you will   199
make some money by the end of the day!   208

GO ON

Comprehension and Vocabulary Questions

1. *What are yard sales?* (Yard sales are events where you set up tables outdoors and sell things you no longer want or need.)

2. *Why should you put items on <u>display</u> in groups?* (Putting similar things together in groups helps people find things they might want to buy.)

3. *What can you do to help sell more things at a yard sale?* (Hang up signs so more people know about the sale, lower prices, and put your things into groups.)

Fluency Score	Comprehension / Vocabulary Score	How to Score Questions
Total words correctly read in 30 seconds _____ X 2	1._____ 2._____	2 = full credit answer 1 = partial credit answer 0 = incorrect/unanswered
Score _____ Goal 79–99 WCPM	3._____ Score _____/6 Goal = 4/6	

□ **Move Ahead** The student met goals for both sections.

□ **Needs Reteaching** The student did not meet goals for one or both sections.

Mr. Clark's Class

Mr. Clark's class was excited today. The children had made the effort to bring their pets to school. There were three little dogs, one puppy, two cats, two kittens, one parrot, and two goldfish. There was also one lizard, one snake, two hamsters, one turtle, one rabbit, and even one chicken. The animals sat quietly while Mr. Clark talked about each of them.

At lunchtime, the children left the animals in the classroom. As soon as the door was closed, the animals got into trouble. The dogs chased the cats. The hamsters and turtle began eating the children's work. The puppy tried to catch the parrot, and the kittens tried to catch the fish. The rabbit knocked over some paint, and the paint spilled onto the lizard. The snake crawled into Mr. Clark's desk, and the chicken deliberately laid an egg on top of it!

When the class got back from lunch, the children saw what the pets had done. Quickly they began cleaning up the mess. The class was still not satisfied when Mr. Clark walked back in. But he did not notice any of it. The children could not believe that Mr. Clark did not see the mess made by the pets!

Mr. Clark's Class

Mr. Clark's class was excited today. The children   11

had made the effort to bring their pets to school.   21

There were three little dogs, one puppy, two cats,   30

two kittens, one parrot, and two goldfish. There was   39

also one lizard, one snake, two hamsters, one turtle,   48

one rabbit, and even one chicken. The animals sat   57

quietly while Mr. Clark talked about each of them.   66

At lunchtime, the children left the animals in   74

the classroom. As soon as the door was closed, the   84

animals got into trouble. The dogs chased the cats.   93

The hamsters and turtle began eating the children's   101

work. The puppy tried to catch the parrot, and the   111

kittens tried to catch the fish. The rabbit knocked   120

over some paint, and the paint spilled onto the   129

lizard. The snake crawled into Mr. Clark's desk, and   138

the chicken deliberately laid an egg on top of it!   148

When the class got back from lunch, the children   157

saw what the pets had done. Quickly they began   166

cleaning up the mess. The class was still not satisfied   176

when Mr. Clark walked back in. But he did not   186

notice any of it. The children could not believe that   196

Mr. Clark did not see the mess made by the pets!   207

GO ON

Comprehension and Vocabulary Questions

1. *What happens in the classroom at lunchtime?* (The pets in Mr. Clark's class make a mess in the classroom.)

2. *Why is the class surprised when Mr. Clark comes back after lunch?* (He does not seem to notice that the classroom is messy.)

3. *Why wasn't the class* <u>satisfied</u> *when Mr. Clark came back to the classroom?* (The class did not think they had cleaned up all of the mess.)

Fluency Score	**Comprehension / Vocabulary Score**	**How to Score Questions**
Total words correctly read in 30 seconds _____ X 2 Score _____ Goal 79–99 WCPM	1. _____ 2. _____ 3. _____ Score ____ /6 Goal = 4/6	2 = full credit answer 1 = partial credit answer 0 = incorrect/unanswered

☐ **Move Ahead** The student met goals for both sections. | ☐ **Needs Reteaching** The student did not meet goals for one or both sections.